Jared Potter Kirtland

Family History

Genealogy of the Cooke family. An interesting glimpse of early New

England life.

Jared Potter Kirtland

Family History
Genealogy of the Cooke family. An interesting glimpse of early New England life.

ISBN/EAN: 9783744794077

Printed in Europe, USA, Canada, Australia, Japan

Cover: Foto ©ninafisch / pixelio.de

More available books at **www.hansebooks.com**

A FAMILY HISTORY.

GENEALOGY OF THE

COOKE FAMILY.

By Dr. J. P. KIRTLAND.

AN INTERESTING GLIMPSE OF EARLY NEW ENGLAND LIFE.

1875.

COOKE GENEALOGY.

For minute details see Dr. C. H. S. Davis' "*History of Wallingford*," for sale
by J. Munsell, Bookseller, Albany, N. Y. Price, $5.00.
Or Cleveland Historical Society.

The ancestors of most of this name in New England
came from Herefordshire and Kent in England. Henry
Cooke was at Plymouth, Mass., before 1640. His sons,
Isaac is supposed to have remained at Plymouth, and
John to have settled at Middletown, Conn. Henry and
Samuel settled at Wallingford, Conn., and were the ancest-
ors of all the Connecticut Cooke. All were Puritans.

a. SAMUEL,

came to New Haven in 1663, married Hope, daughter of
Edward Parke, in that place, May 2d, 1667. They went
to Wallingford in April, 1667, with the first planters ;
was the first tanner and shoemaker there and was regarded
as a very good man ; was frequently called to fill respon-
sible offices in the church and village. After the decease
of his wife Hope, he married Mary Roberts, July 14th,

1690. He died March, 1702, and left an estate of £340.
By the two marriages he had fifteen children ; the eighth
child we will designate as ISAAC 1st, though he had a son
Isaac who died in his infancy in 1673.

b. ISAAC 1st.

son of Samuel and Hope Cooke, born January 10th, 1681.
Married Sarah Curtis, October 11th, 1705. He died in
Wailingford, February 1st, 1712. Estate, £103. They
had four children ; the fourth was ISAAC COOKE, 2d.

c. ISAAC, 2d.

born July 22d, 1710. Married Jerusha Sexton, of Wol-
lingford, Oct. 15th, 1733. He died March 16th, 1786,
aged 80 years. She died Oct. 13th, 1795. He was a
tanner and currier of leather. CHILDREN : 1. Amos,
born Dec. 5th, 1734 ; 2d. Jerusha, born Nov. 19th, 1736 ;
3d. Isaac 3d, born July 28th, 1739 ; 4th. Caleb, born
Nov. 14th, 1741 ; 5th. Mindwell, born Dec. 9th, 1743,
died Jan. 26th, 1749 ; 6th. Ambrose, born March 19th,
1744, died in infancy ; Ambrose, born June 30th, 1745 ;
8th. Elihu, born Aug. 16th, 1747, died Aug. 31st, 1747 ;
9th. Mindwell, born April 20th, 1750, married Capt

Jeremiah Carrington and kept the noted "Carrington Hotel" in Wallingford for many years, and as late as the year 1812.

d. AMOS,

son of Isaac 2d and Jerusha Cooke, married Rhoda Hosford. CHILDREN : 1. *Elihu*, born April 25th, 1757 ; 2. *Rhoda*, born April 16th, 1761, married John Davis ; 3. *Roswell*, born Dec. 6th, 1764 ; 4. *Uri H.*, born Jan. 19th, 1767, supposed to have settled in Norway, Herkimer Co., N.Y., in 1798 ; 5. *Amos*, born Nov. 29, 1768 ; 6. *Lucinda*, born Oct. 31, 1771, married Stephan Hart in 1790 ; 7. *Sybil*, born Oct. 10th, 1778, married Thomas Welton, Jan. 3d, 1797 ; 8. *Lyman*, born Sept. 21, 1780, settled at Marcellus, N. Y.; 9. *Desire*, born March 5th, 1783.

Of the children of Isaac and Jerusha Cooke (Isaac 2d) there settled and were living in Wallingford, as late as 1810, the following, to-wit :

1. Amos.   4. Ambrose.
2. Isaac 3d.   5. Mindwell.
3. Caleb.

d. AMOS.

Long before the American Revolution, he attached himself to the then small society of Episcopalians. That society were Loyalists or Tories at and during the Revolution. Small in numbers they embraced some of the best families in that town. A most violent and virulent persecution was commenced against them, not milder nor more tolerant than the recent Ku Klux at the South. Many of the best families were compelled to flee with their clergyman, the Rev. Samuel Andrews, to Nova Scotia. Amos Cooke took a prominent position in defense of his religious rights. A history of the insults, abuses, and persecutions he suffered during that contest would fill a volume. I have heard them recounted a thousand times over by himself, his friends and foes. Arrests and fines used up all his property and destroyed his business. At the close of the war he was poor but owned a small place on Main street, in Wallingford.

In 1786-7 the constitution of the United States was formed and adopted. He once told me that he now, as during the revolution, *"was determined to be on*

the side of the Government," and accordingly attached himself to the Federal party as an ardent defender of the new constitution. All of the Episcopalians in that town, as well as many of its best people, took the same position, but all of that numerous rabble that had been such ardent patriots during the revolution now became anti-Federalists or Democrats. Many respectable persons also joined the anti-Federal party, which constituted a large majority in the town. Politics never ran higher or raged with more virulence.

They eventuated in the election of Mr. Jefferson as president. The great Jeffersonian festival was held here on the 11th of March, 1801.

" *Physical causes influence the moral faculty*," wrote Dr. Rush. Both physical and mental causes had for a long series of years exerted their full and unfavorable influences on this individual and changed his nature and disposition. While the whole Cooke family, in all its branches, were distinguished for kindness, affability, and a musical taste, he from 1800 to 1810, when I intimately knew him was morose, misanthropic and quarrelsome. This life of controversy had obliterated the kind

.

Cooke disposition and substituted a pugilistic one in its place. His children scattered and left him, and he and his wife, for at least ten years experienced a life of poverty, relieved in part by the contributions of his son Roswell, his Cooke relations, and the members of the Episcopal church.

His wife died May 10th, 1810. Soon after Roswell came with a carriage and prepared to take his father to Farmington, where he would be well cared for. Persuasion make no impression. "*No*," said he, "*I'd rather stay here and read Hudson & Goodwin,*" (the Federal newspaper) *then to go and live with my son Roswell.*" Two of the township selectmen thought to hasten a termination of the affair by raising him by force into the carriage. A demonstration on his part soon convinced them that their line of duty lay in some other direction. He, however, soon after left Wallingford and took up his residence among his children. From his granddaughter, Mrs. Rachel Pomeroy Emmet, I learn that he died at the house of his youngest son, *Lyman Cooke,* in Marcellus, N. Y., in the year 1813, age over eighty years.

Mrs. Emmet was in error in supposing her grand-

mother to have died when her son, Roswell, was a child. Her youngest child, Desire, was born in 1783, when Roswell was nineteen years old. Dr. Davis' Genealogy says, that she died on the 10th of May, 1810. I think I distinctly recollect the event on the day I left Wallingford on my first visit to Ohio.

f. ROSWELL.

The 3d son of Amos and Rhoda Hosford Cooke, born December 6th, 1764, married Rachel Newell, of Southington, Conn., October 21st, 1788, died in Delaware, O., on December 27th, 1827. At the age of sixteen years he volunteered into the army of the revolution, where he continued till the end of that contest, when he was honorably discharged. He purchased a farm on the rich interval lands in the township of Farmington, where he resided till 1813. He was a very respectable citizen, and one of the best farmers in the vicinity. It was a singular coincidence that while his father, *Amos Cooke*, was suffering persecution in the town of Wallingford for his rigid Episcopalian views and his Federal beliefs, that his son Roswell's residence in Farmington was rendered unpleasant

and even uncomfortable by the treatment he received from the population of that town. Roswell Cooke was an extensive reader for a farmer, was in politics a firm Jeffersonian Democrat, and his religious views did not square with those of the Saybrook platform, entertained by the good people of Farmington. From these circumstances constant bickerings arose, till, in the year 1813, while the war with Great Britain was progressing, they became so unpleasant that he sold his fine farm on the Farmington intervals and removed to Columbus, Ohio. Here he located on a fine farm between that city and Worthington, in the vicinity of the Scioto river.

CHILDREN:

1. *Chauncey.*

2. *Rodney*, married Laura Cowles at Farmington; removed to Ohio with his father in 1813.

3. *Philecta*, married Judge Ezra Griswold and settled in Delaware, O.; is now a widow in Brooklyn, N.Y.

4. *Rachel Pomeroy*, married first Wm. Converse; he died. She then married the Rev. Wm. Y. Emmet. She died at Springfield, Clarke Co., O., in 1874.

.

5. *Justin*, married Maria Watson, of Chillicothe ; died only six weeks after. Was a promising young lawyer.

6. *Jennett*, married Joseph Howard, lawyer, and settled at Tiffin, O. She is now a widow in New York.

g. CHAUNCEY, 7

born in Farmington, Conn., 1789, married in the same town Caroline Gridley, September 1st, 1812. In the autumn of 1810 Chauncey Cooke entered the popular and flourishing academy at Wallingford, then in charge of the Rev. Joshua Bradley. At that time a very pleasant, intelligent and social circle of young people were either in attendance on the academy or were residents of the town. Sleighrides, balls, and especially cotillion parties, under the direction of Nathan Clark, afterward colonel in the United States army, frequently engaged the attention of that social circle. Young Cooke was a popular member of it, and as it often engaged in vocal music, and he was a proficient as a singer, he became our musical leader. At that day "*Jefferson and Liberty*," though now forgotten, was then the universal party song

of the Jeffersonians. Politics ran high and it was frequently sang by our young circle. Cooke generally officiated as chorister on such occasions.

In 1813 I learned incidentally that he and all of Roswell Cooke's family had left Farmington and gone to the west, but to what point did not hear, nor did I ever hear anything of him for more than half a century. Fifty-three years afterward he, totally unexpected, called on me at my residence, near Cleveland. Subsequently we often met, talked over the events of our days of early life, and sang together the song of "Jefferson and Liberty." What a change had that long interval of time effected with both of us. He died March 1st, 1875, at the residence of his youngest daughter, Mrs. J. Barber, in Cleveland, O., aged eighty-five years. His remains were taken to his old home, near Columbus for interment.

Divergence of the Mrs. President Hayes Branch of the Cooke Family.

Isaac Cooke, third child of Isaac and Jerusha Sexton Cooke, Wallingford, Conn., born July 28th, 1739 (brother of Amos). At the age of nineteen he had completed his common school education, what then embraced reading, spelling, writing, and arithmetic, and was engaged in learing the trade of stone mason and working at intervals on a farm. At this age he was distinguished for his muscular strength and activity. Athletic exercises, as wrestling, running, jumping, etc., were the popular amusements of the young men. At these he was universally the victor in all contests. Even as late as the year of his death, 1810, his step was as firm and precise as the best drilled West Point student. In 1758, a requisition was made on the province of Connecticut for a large body of her militia to join the expedition against Canada, fitting out under General Abercrombie. Scores of young men, Isaac Cooke among the number, were pressed (not drafted), and forth-

with joined the army before Ticonderoga. They were placed under the tyrannical instruction of the British drill sergeants, and from necessity became military proficients. He was present at the battle when Lord Howe was killed. At the close of the campaign he was discharged and returned home, thoroughly embued with martial experience, and was soon elected captain of one of the Wallingford militia companies, an unusual compliment to be conferred on so young a man in those days. This position he held till the commencement of the American revolution, and he brought his company into the highest state of discipline.

He married Martha, daughter of Benjamin Cooke, March 6th, 1760, and continued to follow his stone mason trade and to carry on farming till the news of the battle of Lexington arrived. On the receipt of that intelligence he and part of his militia company hastened to Boston. As soon as the Provincial Congress formed a regular army he was commissioned a captain. In that army he continued to serve every day during the protracted contest, and at its disbandonment he was honorably discharged as colonel. He was present generally under the immediate command of Washington in several important battles.

At the crossing of the Delaware, and during the ensuing battle, he and his company occupied a most important position.

After the close of that war he resumed his trade and resided on his farm on the crest of Long Hill, in Wallingford, where he died June 10th, 1810, aged seventy-one years. He was universally respected and beloved by a large circle of acquaintances.

CHILDREN—First, Joel, born October 12th, 1760. When his father was appointed captain in the regular army its regulations required captains to be provided with waiters, who drew regular pay from the Government. This son, though only thirteen years old, his father selected, and he served in that capacity seven years, till the close of the war ; then, without a trade or occupation, he married and settled in New Haven. In 1800 the people of Wallingford formed a fine military company, and Joel Cooke was chosen captain of it, though residing thirteen miles from that town. In a brief time he brought the company into such a high state of discipline as to attract public attention. Mr. Jefferson, in a political freak like our modern Democrats, resolved to demolish the United

States regular army. In 1806, finding the Government
involved in a controversy with Spain, he concluded to
raise a number of regiments of troops. Joel Cooke was
appointed captain in the Tenth Regiment under the command of Colonel Boyd. To that regiment General Har-
rison's preservation from a St. Clair defeat at Tippecanoe
was owing. Captain Cooke and company particularly
distinguished themselves. Soon after ill-health compelled
him to resign. He died at Babylon, on Long Island,
December 10th, 1851, aged 92.

Samuel settled at Lewiston, N.Y., in 1793. Was
father of Bates Cooke, who was for many years Comp-
troller of the treasury of the state of New York.

Isaac 4th, born in Wallingford, Conn., July 16th, 1763,
died at Chillicothe, O., January 22d, 1844 ; the third son
of Colonel Isaac and Martha Cooke. He emigrated to
Chillicothe, O., in 1791, where he was very generally and
favorably known, and in early days filled several public
offices. For a time he was Associate Judge of the Court
of Common Pleas. In the year 1828 I was a member of
the House of Representatives of Ohio, when he, with
Isaac Walk, represented the county of Ross in the same

body. We spent many a pleasant evening together during the winter of 1828-9, during the session of the legislature at Columbus. The early history of our native town of Wallingford and the biography of his numerous Cooke relatives were the principal topics of our conversations. In 1792 he married Margaretta Scott.

Marietta, daughter of Isaac Cooke 4th, married James Webb, M. D. A daughter of this marriage is the wife of Rutherford B. Hayes, president of the United States. Mrs. Hayes descended through four successive generations of Isaac Cookes. Not one of her relatives by the name of Cooke is now to be found in the town of Wallingford. A few distant collateral relations still exist there.

Divergence of the Jay Cooke branch of the Cooke
Family, via the children of Samuel, the brother
of Isaac 1st.

SAMUEL,

the son of Samuel and Hope Cooke, married Hannah
Ives of New Haven, March 3d, 1692. She died May 29,
1714. He then married Elizabeth Bedel, of Stratford.
He died Sept. 18th, 1725, at Wallingford. He was a
farmer in the western part of the township, near the line
which now divides Cheshire from Wallingford. He had
14 children, four by second marriage, of which Asaph
was third.

ASAPH,

son of Samuel and Elizabeth Cooke, married Sarah Parker
of Wallingford and went to Granville, Mass., where he
remained until about the close of the revolution, when
he removed to Granville, N. Y., where he died in 1792.
She died in 1818, aged 96 years. They had 10 children,
the 3d Asaph, b. March 6th, 1748.

ASAPH 2d.

son of Asaph and Sarah Parker Cooke, married Thankful Parker, June 17th, 1776. She was born in Wallingford. They removed to Granville, N. Y., in 1818. They then went to Ridgefield Four Corners, Ohio, where he died in 1826, aged 78 years. He was at the battle of Lexington, as were several of his brothers. His widow died in 1818. There were 12 children, the 6th was *Elutheras*, born December 25th, 1787.

ELUTHERAS,

son of Asaph and Thankful Parker Cooke, married Martha Caswell, of Salem, Washington Co., N. Y. He was a lawyer in Washington Co., before his removal to Sandusky, Ohio. He was frequently a member of the Ohio Legislature and was a member of congress from 1831 to 1833. He died at Sandusky, O., Dec. 27th, 1864.

CHILDREN :

1. *Sarah E.*, born January 16th, 1816.
2. *Pitt*, born July 23d, 1819.
3. *Jay*, born Aug. 10th, 1821. Banker in Philadelphia.

4. *Henry D.*, born Nov. 25th, 1825, now in Washington.
5. *Eluthcras*, born December 20th, 1828.
6. *Catherine E.*, born Sept. 15th, 1831.

꙼ ꙼ ꙼ ꙼

TWENTY-TWO years ago, DR. JARED P. KIRTLAND wrote this account of the branch of the Cooke Family of Wallingford, Conn., for me. Shortly after this Dr. Kirtland died. My wish is to carry on this work a few steps further and to give a brief statement of the facts connected with the family of CHAUNCEY COOKE and his descendants.

Chauncey, first son of Roswell and Rachel Newell Cooke, was born at Farmington, Conn., August 9, 1789. On Sept 1, 1812, he was married to Caroline Gridley, who was born at Farmington, Conn., Sept. 4, 1789. In 1813 they moved to Ohio, where they spent the remainder of their lives, and where their nine children were born to them. Here Caroline Gridley, wife of Chauncey Cooke, died Feb. 10th, 1853.

Their children were:

Catherine Cooke, born in Franklin Co., Ohio, Sept. 3th, 1813—died Feb. 6th, 1875.

Richard H. Cooke, born in Franklin Co., Ohio, Jan. 28th, 1815—died May 20th, 1835.

John Pomeroy Cooke, born in Franklin Co., Ohio, March 9, 1817—died January 19th, 1874.

Samuel S. Cooke, born in Franklin Co., Ohio, Dec. 9th, 1818—died April 12, 1879.

Theodore Newell Cooke, born in Franklin Co., Ohio, Nov. 15th, 1820—died Oct. 6th, 1865.

Chauncey C. Cooke, born in Franklin Co., Ohio, Nov. 30th. 1832—died June 28th, 1877.

Justin Oscar Cooke, born in Franklin Co., Ohio, Jan. 19, 1825—died August 30, 1847.

Caroline Jennette Cooke, born in Franklin Co., Ohio, January 28, 1827.

Maria Felicity, born May 6, 1830—died Aug. 22, 1831.

Caroline Jennette Cooke, born in Franklin Co., Jan. 28, 1827, married Josiah Barber, Civil Engineer, of Cleveland, Ohio, Jan. 16, 1851. They spent some years of their married life on the old farm in Franklin County. Here was born to them, on July 6, 1852, their only child, Kate Cooke Barber, who died here June 6th, 1863.

When the war broke out, Mr. Barber enlisted and served three years in the 95th Ohio Inf. Reg't as first lieutenant, and served to the end of the war. At the close of the war, Mr. and Mrs. Barber moved to Cleveland, here in 1884 Mr. Barber died, aged 59 years.

I have added these few personal notes to the account written by Dr. Kirtland. Any member of the family wishing to carry on the work further, may do it, as it pleases him.

Never was there a family more kind and genial among themselves than this branch of the Cookes. They were open hearted and hospitable, and several of them quite gifted in a musical way, so that the home became the natural gathering place for people all around the country on all sorts of festive occasions.

I am the last living child of Chauncey Cooke, my
ild and husband have also gone before me, so it is for
e children of my brothers and sisters, and their cousins,
at this account will be of interest, and it is for their
easure that I have put it into this shape.

MRS. JOSIAH BARBER.

July 7, 1897.

1620731

Of the children of Roswell and Rachel Newell Cooke,
hauncey and Rodney settled on the old farm on the
Worthington Road, where they each had nine children
orn to them; living near together, the children were
iised almost as one family. They had large business
nterprises for those days, grist mills, saw mills, etc.,
esides farming. Of these large families two of Rodney's
emain. H. C. Cooke living on the old farm, Demmon P.
Cooke in Columbus, Ohio, and one of Chauncey's, Mrs.
Caroline J. Barber, of Cleveland, Ohio.

This history would be incomplete did I not touch a
ittle on pioneer life in the early days of Ohio. My
grandfather, with his family, his sons Chauncey and Rodney, with their young wives, were six weeks coming from

their pleasant home in Connecticut to their future home in Ohio. At that time there was one log cabin where Columbus now stands. The site of the future city was a *slashing*; in after years we children often laughed with our parents over their experiences, especially their long journey from Connecticut, which they never tired of narrating. One great trial they met with was the Pennsylvania wagons with their six horse teams and drivers. Sometimes it amounted to a *skirmish* (when they attempted to take the right of way from the " *damned Yankee carts*, as they termed the two-horse wagons from Connecticut) in which case they always found if the carts were small they carried plenty of *muscle*, and the muscle carried the day. They had the good fortune to arrive safely at their destination, with plenty of strength and energy to carry on their work in the new country.

MRS. JOSIAH BARBER,
Cleveland, Ohio.

www.ingramcontent.com/pod-product-compliance
Lightning Source LLC
Chambersburg PA
CBHW032133080426
42733CB00008B/1051